VICE CREAM

"Many people who have shifted to a healthy plant-based diet have told me that the hardest food for them to do without is quality ice cream. Now, thanks to Jeff Rogers, you can make your own gourmet frozen desserts without dairy products. And they'll taste better than Ben & Jerry's or Baskin-Robbins ever did!"

—John Robbins,
author of *Diet for a New America* and *The Food Revolution*

"The vice cream was quite delicious. . . . We enjoyed the taste test and felt honored to be among the first to try this exciting cruelty-free dessert. We are all nut lovers, so the maple walnut was a huge hit. We loved the chocolate chip too, especially the way the chips are like tiny morsels that go through every spoonful, making each bite totally tasty."

—Ingrid E. Newkirk,
president of People for the Ethical Treatment of Animals (PETA)

"Sinfully sumptuous, fun to make, and all vegan! That's one improvement in ice cream that's long overdue."

—Dr. Neal Barnard,
president of Physicians Committee for Responsible Medicine

"When it comes to his vice cream recipes, Jeff Rogers has made an impressive addition to the world of delicious, healthy desserts that adds pleasure to our life without the need for artery-clogging cholesterol and saturated fat. Jeff's recipes are simply and sinfully great."

—Francis Janes, international restaurateur

"Jeff Rogers doesn't just give you a slice, but a whole spoonful of heaven with his amazing frozen dessert recipes. His creations are delicious and unforgettable. Yum!"

—Sabrina Nelson, Webwitch, VegSource.com

VICE
Cream

Over 70 Sinfully Delicious
Dairy-Free Delights

Jeff Rogers
The Naughty Vegan!

CELESTIAL ARTS
Berkeley | Toronto

ℂ𝔸

Celestial Arts
Box 7123
Berkeley, California 94707
www.tenspeed.com

Distributed in Australia by Simon and Schuster Australia, in Canada by Ten Speed
Press Canada, in New Zealand by Southern Publishers Group, in South Africa by
Real Books, and in the United Kingdom and Europe by Airlift Book Company.

Cover and text design by Betsy Stromberg

Library of Congress Cataloging-in-Publication Data
Rogers, Jeff, 1961–
    Vice cream : over 70 sinfully delicious dairy-free delights / Jeff Rogers.
        p. cm.
    ISBN 1-58761-199-6 (pbk.)
    1. Ice cream, ices, etc. 2. Vegan cookery. I. Title.
    TX795.R585 2004
    641.5'636—dc22
                                                2003018614

Printed in the United States of America
First printing, 2004

1 2 3 4 5 6 7 8 9 10 — 08 07 06 05 04

CONTENTS

Vice Creams

Raw Vice Creams

Sauces

About the Author ✦

Index ✦

ACKNOWLEDGMENTS

Thanks to Zel and Reuben Allen for all of your help and guidance. As someone who rarely uses recipe books, I appreciate the time and effort you offered to help bring my recipe book to fruition.

Thank you to my mother, Dottie; my brothers, Paul and Sam; and all of my friends and relatives for your support on this project.

A very special thanks goes to Bill Amey, my good friend and co-founder of SoyStache.com, for your continued support, your friendship, and especially your sense of humor.

Thanks to the wonderful staff at Celestial Arts.

And thank you to all who dedicate their lives to helping others improve theirs, whether through diet or otherwise.

INTRODUCTION

In my younger years, I consumed a lot of ice cream and favored the rich flavors of Ben & Jerry's, whose factory happened to be in the neighboring town. After I discovered the benefits of a vegan diet, I found that the vegan "ice creams" on the market were simply not satisfying; they were not rich enough, and they seemed to have an unpleasant aftertaste.

Since there are many people who cannot eat dairy and many more who choose not to for ethical, environmental, and health reasons, I wanted to create a wonderful ice cream alternative. For those who were already vegans, this would add a new dessert to their diets. For others, it would allow them to give up the dairy they had been wanting to do without.

I thought that there must be a way of making a rich, flavorful vegan ice cream that would easily satisfy the expectations I had developed when I ate dairy. Having used cashew milk to replace cow's milk and cream in other recipes, I realized that was how I should make my homemade vegan ice cream. In 1999, I moved to Seattle, purchased an ice cream maker, and began experimenting with vegan ice creams. The results were as rich as I wanted them to be. "Vice cream" was finally born!

I began sharing my vice cream at local EarthSave potlucks and at other EarthSave chapters in cities like Vancouver, Canada; Portland, Oregon; and San Diego, California. I soon had many people asking for my recipes or for the vice cream itself. Over time, I've traveled to many vegan, raw, and health food shows to demonstrate how delicious vice cream can be and how easy it is to make. Sharing this healthful alternative to dairy ice cream has become part of my life's work.

I soon realized that I'd rather distribute my recipes widely rather than produce vice cream commercially, since using organic cashews, the base for most of the recipes, is rather expensive, and allowing people to make vice cream themselves would make it more affordable. I believe that these recipes will make a difference in people's lives. I certainly hope they succeed in doing so.

Basics

Sweeteners

I created the recipes to suit my own taste in sweetness, but feel free to adjust them according to your preference. I love maple syrup and use it as the primary sweetener in my recipes. I prefer Grade A dark fancy maple syrup.

Other sweeteners can be substituted for maple syrup, though those such as Sucanat or dates will change the consistency of the mixture and may require that you thin it with additional liquid. One cup of maple syrup can be substituted with ¾ cup agave nectar, 1½ cups Sucanat, or 1 cup packed organic pitted dates.

For raw vice creams, I prefer to use dates in place of maple syrup. When using dates, I usually select medjool, honey, or sometimes black dates, though other varieties can also be substituted. I've found honey dates to be very versatile, working well in most recipes. Darker dates, like medjool and black dates, have a stronger flavor that works well in some recipes, but they tend to overwhelm vice creams that have subtler flavors. The skins of the dates may produce some speckling in your vice cream; if you wish to avoid this, just remove the skins before blending. Soft dates may be used without soaking, but they might make the vice cream mixture too thick, in which case just add some water.

Dry pitted dates do not work well on their own and generally need soaking. Measure out the dates, then loosen them and transfer them to a jar. Add enough purified water to cover them. Place the jar in the refrigerator, to prevent fermentation, for several hours to overnight. Drain, reserving the sweet soaking liquid. To add extra sweetness, you may want to use the soaking liquid in place of some of the other liquids in a recipe, or you can save it for another use.

Brown rice syrup doesn't have the same sweetening ability as these other ingredients, but it may work well when mixed with another sweetener, such as maple syrup. For those who wish to use brown rice syrup, I suggest mixing brown rice syrup and maple syrup in equal parts, then adjusting to taste.

Diabetics and those who prefer not to use sweeteners that contain sugars can try using stevia, an all-natural dried herb. Some types of stevia, however, have a licorice flavor that overwhelms some recipes. Some stevia powders are still green, and others have been refined. The green type is likely to be more natural, but it has the stronger flavor. Try using about 1½ teaspoons of stevia in place of 1 cup of maple syrup (see the Carob Stevia recipe on page 30). Stevia alone may not be sweet enough, so if you want to try stevia and don't object to the use of other sweeteners, you can use a combination of maple syrup and stevia. This combination offers sweetness with reduced sugars.

For additional sweetness in any recipe, the water can be replaced with fresh juice, such as young coconut water or grape juice.

Juicing

I use a Champion juicer made by Plastaket Manufacturing Company. Green Power also makes a great juicer, known as Green Star. There are many others on the market with varying functions and efficiency. The Champion and Green Star are "masticating" juicers; they chew the food to break down the fibers and squeeze out the juice. Other juicers are centrifugal, with either angled mesh baskets that throw your pulp into a container, or mesh baskets with vertical sides that require periodic cleaning if you're working with a large batch of produce.

If you do not have a juicer, a food mill can be used to purée fruit and remove the skin and seeds, but be aware that the volume and texture of the juice may differ. For example, grape juice from a food mill won't taste the same as grape juice from a juicer, because removing the seeds changes the flavor. Also, because juicers have finer screens, using a food mill may make the juice thicker and may extract less liquid.

Some fruits, such as grapes and apples, can simply be shredded or grated, placed in a fine-mesh bag, and squeezed. For soft fruits, such as strawberries, it may be best to simply use the same amount of packed fruit as the juice called for in the recipe. Although it adds an extra step to your preparation time, you may wish to peel fruits such as peaches before use, as the skins can thicken your mixture too much without adding extra flavor or texture. If your vice cream mixture does turn out too thick, add some liquid, such as purified water.

Extracts

Use only alcohol-free extracts in vice cream recipes, as those with alcohol will inhibit the mixture's ability to freeze. The flavorings I use are available in most health food stores and are actually labeled "flavors," not "extracts." Frontier Natural Products has a nice line of natural flavors.

Vanilla

Natural vanilla flavor and vanilla beans are called for in many of my recipes and can be used interchangeably. When using the beans, I usually include the whole things—pod, seeds, and all. Depending on your taste, you'll need a quarter to one whole vanilla bean for many recipes. Cut the bean into pieces, then grind it to a powder in a clean coffee grinder before adding it to the vice cream mixture. Depending on the ability of your blender, the cut-up bean may be added directly to the blender along with the other ingredients. I also sometimes blend a cut-up bean with some liquid in a 1-cup blender jar before adding it to the larger blender. Using the entire bean, with the pod, is easier, but the vanilla flavor actually comes from the seeds. If you don't want to include the pod, just slice the beans lengthwise and scrape the seeds into the mixture. The overall texture will be slightly smoother without the pod.

Chocolate Chips

I prefer smaller chocolate chips than those commonly available, and I've tried a variety of methods—food processors, coffee grinders, and even manual grinders—for creating the ideal chips for my recipes. The trick is to break the chocolate into smaller pieces without the heat from the process melting the chips. What seems to work best is to chill the bowl and slicing blade of a food processor in the freezer, and then use them to process room-temperature chips. When I've chilled the chips, they've been too hard to properly slice. Even with this method, I end up with chips of various sizes. If you don't have a food processor, use a knife and cutting board to chop the chips. Or, if you find a good bulk vegan chocolate or even a vegan chocolate bar, you can grate it with a hand grater.

Before adding chocolate chips to your vice cream recipe, always chill them in your freezer for at least fifteen minutes.

Ginger Juice

To make fresh ginger juice, either pass peeled fresh ginger through a juicer, press it in a garlic press, or grate and squeeze it. In a pinch, you can also use plain grated ginger, grated using the smallest holes possible. I usually make up a large batch of juice in my juicer and then freeze it for future use. Six ounces of fresh ginger will yield about three ounces of juice, or about six tablespoons.

Nut Milks

Raw vice creams call for the use of nut milks, such as almond and hazelnut milk. I use a juicer to produce the nut milk, but a fine-mesh bag can also be used. This method takes some extra effort, but it works well. When using a juicer to make nut milks, you can also pour the milk through a fine-mesh bag to achieve a smoother texture.

To make 4 cups of **almond milk,** soak 5½ cups raw organic almonds overnight in enough water to cover, plus another third. The next day, drain and rinse the nuts. Using a sturdy blender or food processor, purée the nuts with 5 cups purified water until smooth. If necessary to keep your blender moving, add some additional water. Pass the mixture through a juicer or a fine-mesh bag. (Depending upon the juicer, you may need to feed the pulp through a second time to extract all the milk.) Measure out the amount needed for the recipe, reserving the remainder for another use.

To make **hazelnut milk,** replace the almonds with 5 cups raw organic hazelnuts.

To make **pecan milk,** replace the almonds with 4 cups raw pecans and purée the nuts with only 4 cups purified water.

Coconut Water

Coconut water is the liquid drained from the inside of fresh coconuts, with no alterations. It can be found in both young and mature coconuts, with slightly different flavors. Be sure to read the recipes carefully; some call for coconut milk (see below), others for coconut water.

Coconut Milk

Juicing the meat of mature coconuts is the best way to achieve an amazingly decadent coconut milk, though of course canned coconut milk can also be used. Unlike coconut water, which comes directly from the coconut, coconut milk requires some preparation. It may be substituted, in part or in full, for the cashews and water in my recipes.

To make 4 cups of coconut milk, you'll need about 7 cups of shredded coconut (2 large coconuts) and 3 cups of coconut water. The easiest way to shred the coconut meat is in a food processor. Stop the machine and scrape down the sides of the bowl occasionally as you process the coconut for about three minutes.

Once you have shredded the coconut meat, combine it with the coconut water in a blender and pulse until fairly smooth. If your blender does not have a pulse setting, turn it on and off periodically. Add more coconut water if your blender has difficulty blending the mixture.

To juice the pulp manually, place the mixture in a fine-mesh bag and squeeze the milk out. To juice the pulp mechanically, run it through a juicer two or three times, to make sure you extract all of the milk.

If mature coconuts are not available or are too difficult to use because of the hard shells and meat, you still don't have to use canned canned coconut milk. Young coconuts are not as rich and flavorful as mature coconuts, but they are easier to use and offer some of the flavor. Replace the coconut milk in the recipe with a blended mix of young coconut meat and young coconut water. The ratio should be about one part coconut meat to three parts coconut water.

After making your vice cream, you can drink any extra coconut milk straight or add it to a smoothie. If you compost, you should know that coconut shells, mature or young, don't break down very quickly. If you have a fireplace or enjoy campfires, try throwing the shells into the fire (it's fun to watch them burn because they flare up and offer subtle color changes). You need to dry out young coconut shells first, as they have moist husks, so leave them out in the sun for a few days.

Toasted Coconut

To prepare toasted coconut, place a sauté pan over medium heat. Pour 1 to 2 teaspoons of sunflower oil into the pan. When the oil is hot, toss in 1 cup of shredded, unsweetened coconut. Stirring constantly with a wooden spoon, heat until the coconut is light golden brown, being careful not to burn it. If the coconut starts browning too fast, remove the pan from the heat and keep stirring. When browned, transfer it to a plate to cool. Store the toasted coconut in an airtight container in the freezer so that it's chilled and ready to use in a vice cream recipe.

Durian

One of the vice cream recipes calls for durian, a fruit from Southeast Asia that can be found in many Asian grocery stores and other markets that carry exotic fruits. It's shipped to the United States frozen, so you may find it in the freezer section. Durian is a large, thorny, hard-skinned fruit containing four to five sections of fleshy fruit, each enclosing several large seeds. A seven-pound durian will yield about two and a half pounds of edible fruit. When the fruit is ripe and at room temperature, you can pull apart some of the thorns to create a tear in the skin, exposing the fruit within. Be careful, as the thorns are sharp and can cut skin. You can also cut the durian open with a knife, which is a little safer. Be warned that durian is also called "stinky fruit." It has a very distinctive odor, sometimes mistaken for natural gas.

Blending Tips

Before freezing, the consistency of your vice cream mixture should be somewhere between a cream and a thin pudding. It's important that the mixture be very smooth, so add a minute or two to the suggested blending time if your mixture is still gritty. Another way to ensure a smooth texture is to first blend the nuts with a minimal amount of liquid to get them very smooth, then gradually add the remaining liquid called for in the recipe.

You can also soak the nuts overnight in purified water to soften them, which will help them blend more smoothly. If you soak the nuts, cut back slightly on the water or other liquid used in the recipe to maintain the proper consistency. Soaking the nuts may alter the flavor slightly.

Many of these vice cream mixtures, especially those used to make raw vice creams, are quite thick. If your blender seems to have trouble with the nuts or you are not getting good results, try chopping the nuts in a food processor or by hand before adding them to the blender. You can also run the nuts through a masticating juicer with a blank screen to make a nut butter before blending. Also helpful is starting and stopping the blender to loosen up the ingredients around the blade.

Most of the sauce recipes at the end of the book call for a 1-cup blender jar, which is placed upside-down to fit over your traditional blender. It isn't required, but it does a better job of mixing thick ingredients in small quantities because it's smaller than a standard blender jar.

Ice Cream Makers

There are a variety of ice cream makers available on the market. There are two main types of makers: traditional salt-and-ice ice cream makers and newer makers that contain built-in coolant. Traditional ice cream makers, which use salt and ice as coolant, typically have a four- or six-quart capacity, so for large batches, they are the way to go. Manual makers need to be cranked, so they require a lot of physical exertion, while electric are a lot easier to use.

Ice cream makers with built-in coolant need to be placed in the freezer to chill overnight before using. I just store mine in there, so it'll always be ready for the next batch of vice cream. You then take out the ice cream maker, put in the blade and the motor, add your mixture to the canister, and turn it on. This is a very simple way to make a quart of vice cream, since it doesn't require the extra salt and ice, nor does it require a lot of attention or work. These makers are also available with manual cranks.

Serving Instructions

It's always best to serve your vice cream right after making it, if possible. If the vice cream has been stored in the freezer, you'll need to let it rest at room temperature for ten minutes or more before serving it. Vice cream tends to freeze fairly hard and tastes best when softened a bit.

Storage

The fresher the vice cream the better it is, of course, although I've had pints in the freezer that were still tasty after several months. When packing your vice cream into storage containers, try not to leave too much air, which creates frost. Consider using multiple small containers, so that you can empty one container in a sitting and leave full containers for later.

Raw Foods

I've included an entire section devoted to raw vice creams for raw foodists. Since most cashews are heated during the shelling process, some raw foodists will not eat them. Some truly raw cashews (shelled mechanically) are available via mail order, though they are pricey. If you can eat raw cashews, then you will be able to adapt some of the non-raw recipes as well. Or you can try using some almond milk (page 10), fresh coconut milk (page 11), hazelnut milk (page 10), or a combination as a substitute.

To adapt the non-raw vice cream recipes you'll also need to substitute another sweetener for the maple syrup. I recommend soft pitted dates or soaked dry pitted dates (see page 6) in the raw recipes, but raisin or grape juice can also be used for sweetening. Naturally, raw foodists won't be able to use some of the other ingredients, such as chocolate.

A list of online sources for ingredients and equipment for making vice cream can be found at **www.TheNaughtyVegan.com**.

VICE
Creams

Vanilla Delight

MAKES ABOUT 1 QUART

2 vanilla beans
2 cups organic cashews or cashew pieces
2 cups purified water
1 cup maple syrup

Cut the vanilla beans into small pieces. Grind to a fine powder in a clean coffee grinder.

Combine the ground vanilla, cashews, water, and syrup in a blender. Blend on high until silky smooth, at least 1 minute.

Place the blender in the freezer for 40 minutes to 1 hour or in the refrigerator for at least 1 hour or up to overnight, until well chilled. Pour the mixture into an ice cream maker and freeze according to the manufacturer's instructions. Serve immediately or transfer to airtight containers and store in the freezer until ready to serve.

Chocolate

1¾ cups organic cashews or cashew pieces
1¾ cups purified water
1 cup maple syrup
2 teaspoons alcohol-free vanilla flavor
¼ teaspoon alcohol-free almond flavor
½ cup unsweetened cocoa powder

Combine the cashews, water, syrup, vanilla flavor, and almond flavor in a blender. Blend on high until silky smooth, at least 1 minute. With the motor running, add the cocoa powder and blend until evenly distributed.

Place the blender in the freezer for 40 minutes to 1 hour or in the refrigerator for at least 1 hour or up to overnight, until well chilled. Pour the mixture into an ice cream maker and freeze according to the manufacturer's instructions. Serve immediately or transfer to airtight containers and store in the freezer until ready to serve.

Carob Replace the cocoa powder with ½ cup unsweetened carob powder.

Chocolate Mint Add 2 teaspoons alcohol-free peppermint flavor to the blender with the other liquid ingredients.

Carob Mint Replace the cocoa powder with ½ cup unsweetened carob powder and add 2 teaspoons alcohol-free peppermint flavor to the blender with the other liquid ingredients.

Chocolate Chip

MAKES ABOUT 1 QUART

1 cup organic vegan chocolate chips (see page 9), chopped
1½ cups organic cashews or cashew pieces
1½ cups purified water
1 cup maple syrup
1½ teaspoons alcohol-free vanilla flavor
⅛ teaspoon alcohol-free almond flavor

Place the chocolate chips in the freezer to chill.

Combine the cashews, water, syrup, vanilla flavor, and almond flavor in a blender. Blend on high until silky smooth, at least 1 minute.

Place the blender in the freezer for 40 minutes to 1 hour or in the refrigerator for at least 1 hour or up to overnight, until well chilled. Pour the mixture into an ice cream maker and freeze according to the manufacturer's instructions. Remove the cover and blade from the ice cream maker and fold in the chocolate chips, distributing evenly. Serve immediately or transfer to airtight containers and store in the freezer until ready to serve.

Carob Chip Replace the chocolate chips with 1 cup carob chips, chopped.

Mint Chocolate Chip Add 2 teaspoons alcohol-free peppermint flavor to the blender with the other liquid ingredients.

Mint Carob Chip Replace the chocolate chips with 1 cup carob chips, chopped, and add 2 teaspoons alcohol-free peppermint flavor to the blender with the other liquid ingredients.

Chocoholic Delight

MAKES ABOUT 1 QUART

1 cup organic vegan chocolate chips (see page 9), chopped
1½ cups organic cashews or cashew pieces
1½ cups purified water
1 cup maple syrup
1 tablespoon alcohol-free vanilla flavor
½ teaspoon alcohol-free almond flavor
½ cup unsweetened cocoa powder

Place the chocolate chips in the freezer to chill.

Combine the cashews, water, syrup, vanilla flavor, and almond flavor in a blender. Blend on high until silky smooth, at least 1 minute. With the motor running, add the cocoa powder and blend until evenly distributed.

Place the blender in the freezer for 40 minutes to 1 hour or in the refrigerator for at least 1 hour or up to overnight, until well chilled. Pour the mixture into an ice cream maker and freeze according to the manufacturer's instructions. Remove the cover and blade from the ice cream maker and fold in the chocolate chips, distributing evenly. Serve immediately or transfer to airtight containers and store in the freezer until ready to serve.

Carob Delight Replace the chocolate chips with 1 cup carob chips, chopped, and the cocoa powder with ½ cup unsweetened carob powder.

Brownie Chocolate Chip Replace the chocolate chips with 1 cup crumbled vegan chocolate chip brownie.

Chocolate Pecan

MAKES ABOUT 1 QUART

1 cup chopped organic pecans
1½ cups organic cashews or cashew pieces
1½ cups purified water
1 cup maple syrup
2 teaspoons alcohol-free vanilla flavor
¼ teaspoon alcohol-free almond flavor
½ cup unsweetened cocoa powder

Place the pecans in the freezer to chill.

Combine the cashews, water, syrup, vanilla flavor, and almond flavor in a blender. Blend on high until silky smooth, at least 1 minute. With the motor running, add the cocoa powder and blend until evenly distributed.

Place the blender in the freezer for 40 minutes to 1 hour or in the refrigerator for at least 1 hour or up to overnight, until well chilled. Pour the mixture into an ice cream maker and freeze according to the manufacturer's instructions. Remove the cover and blade from the ice cream maker and fold in the pecans, distributing evenly. Serve immediately or transfer to airtight containers and store in the freezer until ready to serve.

Carob Pecan Replace the cocoa powder with ½ cup unsweetened carob powder.

Espresso

1 vanilla bean (optional)
¼ teaspoon alcohol-free almond flavor (optional)
2 cups organic cashews or cashew pieces
2 cups purified water
1 cup maple syrup
2 tablespoons freshly ground organic espresso beans

Cut the vanilla bean into small pieces. Grind into fine powder in a clean coffee grinder.

Combine the ground vanilla, almond flavor, cashews, water, syrup, and ground espresso beans in a blender. Blend on high until silky smooth, at least 1 minute.

Place the blender in the freezer for 40 minutes to 1 hour or in the refrigerator for at least 1 hour or up to overnight, until well chilled. Pour the mixture into an ice cream maker and freeze according to the manufacturer's instructions. Serve immediately or transfer to airtight containers and store in the freezer until ready to serve.

Espresso Mint Add 2 teaspoons alcohol-free peppermint flavor to the blender with the other liquid ingredients.

Mocha

MAKES ABOUT 1 QUART

2 cups organic cashews or cashew pieces
2 cups purified water
1 cup maple syrup
¼ teaspoon alcohol-free almond flavor
4 teaspoons freshly ground organic espresso beans
¼ cup unsweetened cocoa powder

Combine the cashews, water, syrup, almond flavor, and ground espresso beans in a blender. Blend on high until silky smooth, at least 1 minute. With the motor running, add the cocoa powder and blend until evenly distributed.

Place the blender in the freezer for 40 minutes to 1 hour or in the refrigerator for at least 1 hour or up to overnight, until well chilled. Pour the mixture into an ice cream maker and freeze according to the manufacturer's instructions. Serve immediately or transfer to airtight containers and store in the freezer until ready to serve.

Mocha Mint Add 2 teaspoons alcohol-free peppermint flavor to the blender with the other liquid ingredients.

Peanut Butter

1 cup organic cashews or cashew pieces
2 cups purified water
1 cup maple syrup
2 teaspoons alcohol-free vanilla flavor
⅛ teaspoon alcohol-free almond flavor
1 cup smooth natural peanut butter

Combine the cashews, water, syrup, vanilla flavor, and almond flavor in a blender. Blend on high until silky smooth, at least 1 minute. With the motor running, add the peanut butter and blend until evenly distributed.

Place the blender in the freezer for 40 minutes to 1 hour or in the refrigerator for at least 1 hour or up to overnight, until well chilled. Pour the mixture into an ice cream maker and freeze according to the manufacturer's instructions. Serve immediately or transfer to airtight containers and store in the freezer until ready to serve.

Peanut Butter Chocolate Chip After the mixture has frozen, fold in 1 cup chilled organic vegan chocolate chips (see page 9), chopped.

Coconut Macaroon

MAKES ABOUT 1 QUART

1 cup toasted shredded unsweetened coconut (see page 12)
1 cup organic cashews or cashew pieces
1¾ cups coconut milk (see page 11)
1 cup purified water or young coconut water (see page 10)
1 cup maple syrup
2 teaspoons alcohol-free vanilla flavor
⅛ teaspoon alcohol-free almond flavor

Place the toasted coconut in the freezer to chill.

Combine the cashews, coconut milk, water, syrup, vanilla flavor, and almond flavor in a blender. Blend on high until silky smooth, at least 1 minute.

Place the blender in the freezer for 40 minutes to 1 hour or in the refrigerator for at least 1 hour or up to overnight, until well chilled. Pour the mixture into an ice cream maker and freeze according to the manufacturer's instructions. Remove the cover and blade from the ice cream maker and fold in the toasted coconut, distributing evenly. Serve immediately or transfer to airtight containers and store in the freezer until ready to serve.

Chocolate Coconut Macaroon After the ingredients have been blended smooth, add ½ cup unsweetened cocoa powder and blend until evenly distributed.

Coconut Macaroon Chocolate Chip After the mixture has frozen, fold in 1 cup chilled organic vegan chocolate chips (see page 9), chopped.

Almond

MAKES ABOUT 1 QUART

2 cups organic cashews or cashew pieces
2 cups purified water
1 cup maple syrup
1 teaspoon alcohol-free almond flavor

Combine the cashews, water, syrup, and almond flavor in a blender. Blend on high until silky smooth, at least 1 minute.

Place the blender in the freezer for 40 minutes to 1 hour or in the refrigerator for at least 1 hour or up to overnight, until well chilled. Pour the mixture into an ice cream maker and freeze according to the manufacturer's instructions. Serve immediately or transfer to airtight containers and store in the freezer until ready to serve.

Maple Walnut

MAKES ABOUT 1 QUART

1¼ cups chopped organic walnuts
1½ cups organic cashews or cashew pieces
1½ cups purified water
1 cup maple syrup
¼ teaspoon alcohol-free maple flavor

Place the walnuts in the freezer to chill.

Combine the cashews, water, syrup, and maple flavor in a blender. Blend on high until silky smooth, at least 1 minute.

Place the blender in the freezer for 40 minutes to 1 hour or in the refrigerator for at least 1 hour or up to overnight, until well chilled. Pour the mixture into an ice cream maker and freeze according to the manufacturer's instructions. Remove the cover and blade from the ice cream maker and fold in the walnuts, distributing evenly. Serve immediately or transfer to airtight containers and store in the freezer until ready to serve.

Date Nut

MAKES ABOUT I QUART

1 cup chopped organic pecans
1¼ cups organic cashews or cashew pieces
2 cups purified water
¼ cup maple syrup
2 teaspoons alcohol-free vanilla flavor
¼ teaspoon alcohol-free almond flavor
1 cup packed organic pitted medjool dates (see page 6)

Place the pecans in the freezer to chill.

Combine the cashews, water, syrup, vanilla flavor, and almond flavor in a blender. Blend on high until silky smooth, at least 1 minute. With the motor running, gradually add the dates and blend until silky smooth.

Place the blender in the freezer for 40 minutes to 1 hour or in the refrigerator for at least 1 hour or up to overnight, until well chilled. Pour the mixture into an ice cream maker and freeze according to the manufacturer's instructions. Remove the cover and blade from the ice cream maker and fold in the pecans, distributing evenly. Serve immediately or transfer to airtight containers and store in the freezer until ready to serve.

Carob Stevia

2 cups organic cashews or cashew pieces
2¼ cups purified water
1½ teaspoons stevia (see page 7)
1½ teaspoons alcohol-free vanilla flavor
¼ teaspoon alcohol-free almond flavor
1 cup mashed slightly overripe organic banana or other fruit, such as
*   packed hulled organic strawberries (optional)*
½ cup unsweetened carob powder

Combine the cashews, water, stevia, vanilla flavor, and almond flavor in a blender. Blend on high until silky smooth, at least 1 minute. Add the banana and blend until smooth. With the motor running, add the carob powder and blend until evenly distributed.

Place the blender in the freezer for 40 minutes to 1 hour or in the refrigerator for at least 1 hour or up to overnight, until well chilled. Pour the mixture into an ice cream maker and freeze according to the manufacturer's instructions. Serve immediately or transfer to airtight containers and store in the freezer until ready to serve.

Chocolate Stevia Replace the carob powder with ½ cup unsweetened cocoa powder.

Strawberry

MAKES ABOUT 1 QUART

24 ounces fresh organic strawberries, hulled
1½ cups organic cashews or cashew pieces
1 cup maple syrup

Run the strawberries through a juicer to make 2½ cups of juice.

Combine the strawberry juice, cashews, and syrup in a blender. Blend on high until silky smooth, at least 1 minute.

Place the blender in the freezer for 40 minutes to 1 hour or in the refrigerator for at least 1 hour or up to overnight, until well chilled. Pour the mixture into an ice cream maker and freeze according to the manufacturer's instructions. Serve immediately or transfer to airtight containers and store in the freezer until ready to serve.

Blueberry

22 ounces fresh organic blueberries, plus ½ cup chopped blueberries
1 cup organic cashews or cashew pieces
1 cup maple syrup
1 tablespoon alcohol-free vanilla flavor
⅛ teaspoon alcohol-free almond flavor

Run the whole blueberries through a juicer to make 2 cups of juice. (If you don't want to go to the trouble of juicing the blueberries, increase the chopped blueberries to 1 cup, increase the cashews to 1½ cups, and add 1½ cups water. The blueberry taste won't be as intense, but it will still be delicious.)

Combine the blueberry juice, cashews, syrup, vanilla flavor, and almond flavor in a blender. Blend on high until silky smooth, at least 1 minute. Place the blender in the freezer for 40 minutes to 1 hour or in the refrigerator for at least 1 hour or up to overnight, until well chilled.

Place the chopped blueberries in the freezer to chill.

Pour the blueberry juice mixture into an ice cream maker and freeze according to the manufacturer's instructions. Remove the cover and blade from the ice cream maker and fold in the chopped blueberries, distributing evenly. Serve immediately or transfer to airtight containers and store in the freezer until ready to serve.

Raspberry

1½ cups organic cashews or cashew pieces
1½ cups purified water or fresh raspberry juice
1 cup maple syrup
2 teaspoons alcohol-free vanilla flavor
¼ teaspoon alcohol-free almond flavor
1 cup organic raspberries

Combine the cashews, water, syrup, vanilla flavor, and almond flavor in a blender. Blend on high until silky smooth, at least 1 minute. With the motor running, gradually add the raspberries and blend until smooth.

Place the blender in the freezer for 40 minutes to 1 hour or in the refrigerator for at least 1 hour or up to overnight, until well chilled. Pour the mixture into an ice cream maker and freeze according to the manufacturer's instructions. Serve immediately or transfer to airtight containers and store in the freezer until ready to serve.

Banana

1¼ cups organic cashews or cashew pieces
2¼ cups purified water
1 cup maple syrup
1 tablespoon alcohol-free vanilla flavor
1 cup mashed overripe organic banana

Combine the cashews, water, syrup, and vanilla flavor in a blender. Blend on high until silky smooth, at least 1 minute. With the motor running, gradually add the banana and blend until smooth.

Place the blender in the freezer for 40 minutes to 1 hour or in the refrigerator for at least 1 hour or up to overnight, until well chilled. Pour the mixture into an ice cream maker and freeze according to the manufacturer's instructions. Serve immediately or transfer to airtight containers and store in the freezer until ready to serve.

Fresh Lemon

MAKES ABOUT 1 QUART

2 cups organic cashews or cashew pieces
1¼ cups purified water
1 cup maple syrup
¾ cup freshly squeezed lemon juice

Combine the cashews, water, syrup, and lemon juice in a blender.
Blend on high until silky smooth, at least 1 minute.

Place the blender in the freezer for 40 minutes to 1 hour or in the
refrigerator for at least 1 hour or up to overnight, until well chilled.
Pour the mixture into an ice cream maker and freeze according to the
manufacturer's instructions. Serve immediately or transfer to airtight
containers and store in the freezer until ready to serve.

Lemon Increase the water to 2 cups and replace the lemon juice with
6 tablespoons alcohol-free lemon flavor.

Peach Nectar

MAKES ABOUT 1 QUART

2 pounds organic peaches, pitted
1 cup organic cashews or cashew pieces
1 cup maple syrup
1 tablespoon alcohol-free vanilla flavor
⅛ teaspoon alcohol-free almond flavor

Run the peaches through a juicer to make 2½ cups of juice.

Combine the peach juice, cashews, syrup, vanilla flavor, and almond flavor in a blender. Blend on high until silky smooth, at least 1 minute.

Place the blender in the freezer for 40 minutes to 1 hour or in the refrigerator for at least 1 hour or up to overnight, until well chilled. Pour the mixture into an ice cream maker and freeze according to the manufacturer's instructions. Serve immediately or transfer to airtight containers and store in the freezer until ready to serve.

Apple Cinnamon

MAKES ABOUT 1 QUART

3 cups bottled or fresh organic apple juice
1 cup organic cashews or cashew pieces
½ cup maple syrup
4 teaspoons freshly ground cinnamon

Combine the apple juice, cashews, syrup, and cinnamon in a blender. Blend on high until silky smooth, at least 1 minute.

Place the blender in the freezer for 40 minutes to 1 hour or in the refrigerator for at least 1 hour or up to overnight, until well chilled. Pour the mixture into an ice cream maker and freeze according to the manufacturer's instructions. Serve immediately or transfer to airtight containers and store in the freezer until ready to serve.

Strawberry Rhubarb

MAKES ABOUT 1 QUART

12 ounces fresh organic strawberries, hulled
14 ounces fresh organic rhubarb
1½ cups organic cashews or cashew pieces
1 cup maple syrup

Run the strawberries through a juicer to make 1¼ cups of juice. Run the rhubarb through a juicer to make 1¼ cups of juice.

Combine the strawberry juice, rhubarb juice, cashews, and syrup in a blender. Blend on high until silky smooth, at least 1 minute.

Place the blender in the freezer for 40 minutes to 1 hour or in the refrigerator for at least 1 hour or up to overnight, until well chilled. Pour the mixture into an ice cream maker and freeze according to the manufacturer's instructions. Serve immediately or transfer to airtight containers and store in the freezer until ready to serve.

Black Forest

1¾ *pounds organic Bing, Lambert, or Rainier cherries, pitted,*
  plus 1 cup chopped pitted cherries
1 cup organic cashews or cashew pieces
¾ cup maple syrup
¼ teaspoon alcohol-free almond flavor
½ cup unsweetened cocoa powder

Run the 1¾ pounds cherries through a juicer to make 2 cups of juice.

Combine the cherry juice, cashews, syrup, and almond flavor in a blender. Blend on high until silky smooth, at least 1 minute. With the motor running, add the cocoa powder and blend until evenly distributed. Place the blender in the freezer for 40 minutes to 1 hour or in the refrigerator for at least 1 hour or up to overnight, until well chilled.

Place the chopped cherries in the freezer to chill.

Pour the cherry juice mixture into an ice cream maker and freeze according to the manufacturer's instructions. Remove the cover and blade from the ice cream maker and fold in the chopped cherries, distributing evenly. Serve immediately or transfer to airtight containers and store in the freezer until ready to serve.

Peppermint

MAKES ABOUT 1 QUART

1¾ cups organic cashews or cashew pieces
1¾ cups purified water
1 cup maple syrup
2 teaspoons alcohol-free peppermint flavor

Combine the cashews, water, syrup, and peppermint flavor in a
blender. Blend on high until silky smooth, at least 1 minute.

Place the blender in the freezer for 40 minutes to 1 hour or in the
refrigerator for at least 1 hour or up to overnight, until well chilled.
Pour the mixture into an ice cream maker and freeze according to the
manufacturer's instructions. Serve immediately or transfer to airtight
containers and store in the freezer until ready to serve.

Gingersnap
MAKES ABOUT 1 QUART

1¾ cups organic cashews or cashew pieces
1¾ cups purified water
1 cup maple syrup
6 to 8 teaspoons fresh organic ginger juice (see page 9)
3 tablespoons organic blackstrap molasses

Combine the cashews, water, syrup, 6 teaspoons ginger juice, and molasses in a blender. Blend on high until silky smooth, at least 1 minute. Taste the mixture and add up to 2 more teaspoons ginger juice to taste. Blend until evenly distributed.

Place the blender in the freezer for 40 minutes to 1 hour or in the refrigerator for at least 1 hour or up to overnight, until well chilled. Pour the mixture into an ice cream maker and freeze according to the manufacturer's instructions. Serve immediately or transfer to airtight containers and store in the freezer until ready to serve.

Pumpkin

1 cup organic cashews or cashew pieces
1½ cups purified water
1 cup maple syrup
2 tablespoons alcohol-free vanilla flavor
¼ teaspoon alcohol-free almond flavor
3 tablespoons minced fresh organic ginger
1½ teaspoons ground nutmeg
½ teaspoon ground cloves
½ teaspoon ground cinnamon
¼ teaspoon ground allspice
1 cup cooked organic pumpkin or canned organic pumpkin purée

Combine the cashews, water, syrup, vanilla flavor, almond flavor, ginger, nutmeg, cloves, cinnamon, and allspice in a blender. Blend on high until silky smooth, at least 1 minute. With the motor running, add the pumpkin and blend until creamy.

Place the blender in the freezer for 40 minutes to 1 hour or in the refrigerator for at least 1 hour or up to overnight, until well chilled. Pour the mixture into an ice cream maker and freeze according to the manufacturer's instructions. Serve immediately or transfer to airtight containers and store in the freezer until ready to serve

Carrot Cake

2½ pounds organic carrots
½ cup chopped organic walnuts
2 cups organic cashews or cashew pieces
1 cup maple syrup
1 teaspoon alcohol-free vanilla flavor
¼ teaspoon alcohol-free almond flavor
2 teaspoons ground cinnamon
2 teaspoons ground nutmeg
¼ teaspoon ground cloves
⅛ teaspoon ground allspice

Run the carrots through a juicer to make 2 cups of juice. (You can also purée the carrots in a blender and then pass them through a fine-mesh bag and squeeze the juice out.)

Place the walnuts in the freezer to chill.

Combine the carrot juice, cashews, syrup, vanilla flavor, almond flavor, cinnamon, nutmeg, cloves, and allspice in a blender. Blend on high until silky smooth, at least 1 minute.

Place the blender in the freezer for 40 minutes to 1 hour or in the refrigerator for at least 1 hour or up to overnight, until well chilled. Pour the mixture into an ice cream maker and freeze according to the manufacturer's instructions. Remove the cover and blade from the ice cream maker and fold in the walnuts, distributing evenly. Serve immediately or transfer to airtight containers and store in the freezer until ready to serve.

Jalapeño Heaven

MAKES ABOUT 1 QUART

1 to 3 teaspoons minced organic jalapeño chile
2 cups organic cashews or cashew pieces
2 cups purified water
1 cup maple syrup

Combine the jalapeño, cashews, water, and syrup in a blender. Just 1 teaspoon of jalapeño will give the vice cream a slight flavor with a little kick. Adding a second teaspoon will give you more heat, and 3 teaspoons will deliver quite a punch. Blend on high until silky smooth, at least 1 minute.

Place the blender in the freezer for 40 minutes to 1 hour or in the refrigerator for at least 1 hour or up to overnight, until well chilled. Pour the mixture into an ice cream maker and freeze according to the manufacturer's instructions. Serve immediately or transfer to airtight containers and store in the freezer until ready to serve.

Raw VICE Creams

Strawberry

1 vanilla bean
1½ cups almond milk (page 10)
1 cup packed organic pitted honey dates (see page 6)
1½ cups packed hulled organic strawberries

Cut the vanilla bean into small pieces. Grind to a fine powder in a clean coffee grinder.

Combine the ground vanilla, almond milk, dates, and strawberries in a blender. Blend on high until silky smooth, at least 1 minute.

Place the blender in the freezer for 40 minutes to 1 hour or in the refrigerator for at least 1 hour or up to overnight, until well chilled. Pour the mixture into an ice cream maker and freeze according to the manufacturer's instructions. Serve immediately or transfer to airtight containers and store in the freezer until ready to serve.

Strawberry Too

MAKES ABOUT 1 QUART

1¼ pounds fresh organic strawberries, hulled
1 cup young coconut water (see page 10)
½ cup raw organic cashews or cashew pieces
¾ cup packed organic pitted honey dates (see page 6)

Run the strawberries through a juicer to make 2 cups of juice.

Combine the coconut water and cashews in a blender. Blend on high until silky smooth, at least 1 minute. With the motor running, gradually add the strawberry juice and dates and blend until smooth.

Place the blender in the freezer for 40 minutes to 1 hour or in the refrigerator for at least 1 hour or up to overnight, until well chilled. Pour the mixture into an ice cream maker and freeze according to the manufacturer's instructions. Serve immediately or transfer to airtight containers and store in the freezer until ready to serve.

Raw Strawberry Rhubarb

MAKES ABOUT 1 QUART

22 ounces organic rhubarb
½ cup raw organic cashews or cashew pieces
1 cup packed organic pitted honey dates (see page 6)
1 cup packed hulled organic strawberries

Run the rhubarb through a juicer to make 2 cups of juice.

Combine the rhubarb juice and cashews in a blender. Blend on high until silky smooth, at least 1 minute. With the motor running, gradually add the dates and blend until smooth. Add the strawberries and blend until smooth.

Place the blender in the freezer for 40 minutes to 1 hour or in the refrigerator for at least 1 hour or up to overnight, until well chilled. Pour the mixture into an ice cream maker and freeze according to the manufacturer's instructions. Serve immediately or transfer to airtight containers and store in the freezer until ready to serve.

Strawberry Colada

MAKES ABOUT 1 QUART

1¾ pounds organic Sugar Loaf pineapple, peeled and cut into
  1-inch chunks
14 ounces fresh organic strawberries, hulled
1½ cups fresh coconut milk (see page 11)
¾ cup packed organic pitted honey dates (see page 6)

Run the pineapple through a juicer to make 1½ cups of juice. Run the strawberries through a juicer to make 1 cup of juice.

Combine the pineapple juice, strawberry juice, and coconut milk in a blender. Blend on high until silky smooth, at least 1 minute. With the motor running, gradually add the dates, tasting occasionally. When the mixture has achieved the desired sweetness, stop adding the dates and blend until smooth.

Place the blender in the freezer for 40 minutes to 1 hour or in the refrigerator for at least 1 hour or up to overnight, until well chilled. Pour the mixture into an ice cream maker and freeze according to the manufacturer's instructions. Serve immediately or transfer to airtight containers and store in the freezer until ready to serve.

Nectarine

2 cups almond milk (page 10)
½ cup packed organic pitted medjool dates (see page 6)
1½ cups peeled, pitted, and sliced organic nectarines

Combine the almond milk and dates in a blender. Blend on high until silky smooth, at least 1 minute. With the motor running, gradually add the nectarines and blend until smooth.

Place the blender in the freezer for 40 minutes to 1 hour or in the refrigerator for at least 1 hour or up to overnight, until well chilled. Pour the mixture into an ice cream maker and freeze according to the manufacturer's instructions. Serve immediately or transfer to airtight containers and store in the freezer until ready to serve.

Kiwi Mandarin

MAKES ABOUT 1 QUART

2 pounds organic Delite mandarin oranges, peeled and seeded
1¾ pounds organic kiwis, peeled
½ cup packed organic pitted honey dates (see page 6)

Run the mandarins through a juicer to make 1¾ cups of juice. Run the kiwis through a juicer to make 1¾ cups of juice.

Combine the mandarin juice, kiwi juice, and dates in a blender. Blend on high until silky smooth, at least 1 minute.

Place the blender in the freezer for 40 minutes to 1 hour or in the refrigerator for at least 1 hour or up to overnight, until well chilled. Pour the mixture into an ice cream maker and freeze according to the manufacturer's instructions. Serve immediately or transfer to airtight containers and store in the freezer until ready to serve.

Melon Mania

2½ pounds sliced organic honeydew melon or cantaloupe
1 cup raw organic cashews or cashew pieces
½ cup packed organic pitted medjool dates (see page 6)

Run the melon through a juicer to make 3 cups of juice.

Combine the melon juice, cashews, and dates in a blender. Blend on high until silky smooth, at least 1 minute.

Place the blender in the freezer for 40 minutes to 1 hour or in the refrigerator for at least 1 hour or up to overnight, until well chilled. Pour the mixture into an ice cream maker and freeze according to the manufacturer's instructions. Serve immediately or transfer to airtight containers and store in the freezer until ready to serve.

Cranberry

MAKES ABOUT 1 QUART

1½ cups fresh organic cranberries
2 cups purified water
½ cup packed organic pitted honey dates (see page 6)
1 cup mashed overripe organic banana

Combine the cranberries and water in a blender. Blend on high until very smooth, at least 1 minute. Stop the blender and add the dates. Blend until silky smooth. With the motor running, gradually add the banana and blend until creamy.

Place the blender in the freezer for 40 minutes to 1 hour or in the refrigerator for at least 1 hour or up to overnight, until well chilled. Pour the mixture into an ice cream maker and freeze according to the manufacturer's instructions. Serve immediately or transfer to airtight containers and store in the freezer until ready to serve.

Concord Grape

2¼ pounds organic Concord grapes
1 cup raw organic cashews or cashew pieces
½ cup packed organic pitted honey dates (see page 6)

Run the grapes through a juicer to make 3 cups of juice.

Combine the grape juice and cashews in a blender. Blend on high until silky smooth, at least 1 minute. With the motor running, gradually add the dates and blend until smooth.

Place the blender in the freezer for 40 minutes to 1 hour or in the refrigerator for at least 1 hour or up to overnight, until well chilled. Pour the mixture into an ice cream maker and freeze according to the manufacturer's instructions. Serve immediately or transfer to airtight containers and store in the freezer until ready to serve.

Peach

1½ cups coconut water (see page 10)
½ cup raw organic cashews or cashew pieces
2 cups packed sliced organic peaches
½ cup packed organic pitted honey dates (see page 6)

Combine the coconut water and cashews in a blender. Blend on high until silky smooth, at least 1 minute. With the motor running, gradually add the peaches and dates and blend until smooth.

Place the blender in the freezer for 40 minutes to 1 hour or in the refrigerator for at least 1 hour or up to overnight, until well chilled. Pour the mixture into an ice cream maker and freeze according to the manufacturer's instructions. Serve immediately or transfer to airtight containers and store in the freezer until ready to serve.

Blueberry Peach

24 ounces organic blueberries
1¾ pounds organic peaches, pitted
¾ cup packed organic pitted honey dates (see page 6)

Run the blueberries through a juicer to make 1¾ cups of juice. Run
the peaches through a juicer to make 1¾ cups of juice.

Combine the blueberry juice, peach juice, and dates in a blender.
Blend on high until silky smooth, at least 1 minute.

Place the blender in the freezer for 40 minutes to 1 hour or in the
refrigerator for at least 1 hour or up to overnight, until well chilled.
Pour the mixture into an ice cream maker and freeze according to the
manufacturer's instructions. Serve immediately or transfer to airtight
containers and store in the freezer until ready to serve.

Apple Strudel

MAKES ABOUT 1 QUART

1 cup raisins
1¼ pounds organic Fuji apples, plus 1 cup chopped apple
1 cup fresh coconut milk (see page 11)
1 tablespoon freshly ground cinnamon
1 cup chopped organic pecans

Place the raisins in a jar and add enough water to cover. Refrigerate overnight. Drain, reserving the sweet soaking liquid. (To add extra sweetness, you may want to use the soaking liquid in place of some of the coconut water, or you can save it for another use.)

Run the 1¼ pounds apples through a juicer to make 1½ cups of juice.

Combine the apple juice, coconut milk, and cinnamon in a blender. Blend on high until silky smooth, at least 1 minute. Place the blender in the freezer for 40 minutes to 1 hour or in the refrigerator for at least 1 hour or up to overnight, until well chilled.

Place the chopped apple, raisins, and pecans in the freezer to chill.

Pour the apple juice mixture into an ice cream maker and freeze according to the manufacturer's instructions. Remove the cover and blade from the ice cream maker and fold in the chopped apples, raisins, and pecans, distributing evenly. Serve immediately or transfer to airtight containers and store in the freezer until ready to serve.

Banana Lemon

MAKES ABOUT 1 QUART

2½ pounds organic lemons
½ cup packed organic pitted medjool dates (see page 6)
1 cup mashed slightly overripe organic banana
½ cup purified water

Peel the lemons. Separate into sections and remove the membrane and seeds from each section. You should have 2 cups of pulp.

Combine the lemon pulp and dates in a blender. Blend on high until creamy, at least 1 minute. Add the banana and continue blending until creamy. Add enough of the water to make 4 cups total and blend until thoroughly mixed.

Place the blender in the freezer for 40 minutes to 1 hour or in the refrigerator for at least 1 hour or up to overnight, until well chilled. Pour the mixture into an ice cream maker and freeze according to the manufacturer's instructions. Serve immediately or transfer to airtight containers and store in the freezer until ready to serve.

Banana Cherry

MAKES ABOUT 1 QUART

2 cups mashed overripe organic bananas
2 cups packed organic pitted Bing, Lambert, or Rainier cherries

Combine the bananas and 1 cup of the cherries in a food processor fitted with the metal blade. Process until silky smooth, at least 1 minute. Place the food processor bowl in the freezer for 40 minutes to 1 hour or in the refrigerator for at least 1 hour or up to overnight, until well chilled.

Chop the remaining 1 cup cherries and place in the freezer to chill.

Pour the banana-cherry mixture into an ice cream maker and freeze according to the manufacturer's instructions. Remove the cover and blade from the ice cream maker and fold in the chopped cherries, distributing evenly. Serve immediately or transfer to airtight containers and store in the freezer until ready to serve.

Fig

MAKES ABOUT 1 QUART

2 cups fresh coconut milk (see page 11)
1½ cups peeled fresh figs
¾ cup packed organic pitted honey dates (see page 6)

Combine the coconut milk, figs, and dates in a blender. Blend on high until silky smooth, at least 1 minute.

Place the blender in the freezer for 40 minutes to 1 hour or in the refrigerator for at least 1 hour or up to overnight, until well chilled. Pour the mixture into an ice cream maker and freeze according to the manufacturer's instructions. Serve immediately or transfer to airtight containers and store in the freezer until ready to serve.

Coconut Durian

2 cups fresh coconut milk (see page 11), plus more as needed
1¼ cups peeled and seeded durian (see page 12)
¼ cup packed organic pitted honey dates (see page 6)

Combine the coconut milk, durian, and dates in a blender. Blend on high until silky smooth, at least 1 minute. If the mixture seems too thick and is difficult to blend, add additional coconut milk. Blend again until smooth.

Place the blender in the freezer for 40 minutes to 1 hour or in the refrigerator for at least 1 hour or up to overnight, until well chilled. Pour the mixture into an ice cream maker and freeze according to the manufacturer's instructions. Serve immediately or transfer to airtight containers and store in the freezer until ready to serve.

Coconut Cherry

MAKES ABOUT 1 QUART

2 cups fresh coconut milk (see page 11), plus more as needed
2 cups packed organic pitted Bing, Lambert, or Rainier cherries
½ cup packed organic pitted honey dates (see page 6)

Combine the coconut milk, cherries, and dates in a blender. Blend on high until silky smooth, at least 1 minute. If the mixture seems too thick and is difficult to blend, add additional coconut milk. Blend again until smooth.

Place the blender in the freezer for 40 minutes to 1 hour or in the refrigerator for at least 1 hour or up to overnight, until well chilled. Pour the mixture into an ice cream maker and freeze according to the manufacturer's instructions. Serve immediately or transfer to airtight containers and store in the freezer until ready to serve.

Coconut Strawberry

MAKES ABOUT 1 QUART

2 cups fresh coconut milk (see page 11), plus more as needed
1¼ cups packed hulled organic strawberries
¾ cup packed organic pitted honey dates (see page 6)

Combine the coconut milk, strawberries, and dates in a blender. Blend on high until silky smooth, at least 1 minute. If the mixture seems too thick and is difficult to blend, add additional coconut milk. Blend again until smooth.

Place the blender in the freezer for 40 minutes to 1 hour or in the refrigerator for at least 1 hour or up to overnight, until well chilled. Pour the mixture into an ice cream maker and freeze according to the manufacturer's instructions. Serve immediately or transfer to airtight containers and store in the freezer until ready to serve.

Coconut Mango

4 pounds fresh mangoes, peeled and pitted
1¼ cups fresh coconut milk (see page 11)
¾ cup packed organic pitted honey dates (see page 6)

Run the mangoes through a juicer to make 3 cups of juice.

Combine the mango juice and coconut milk in a blender. Blend on high until silky smooth, at least 1 minute. With the motor running, gradually add the dates, tasting occasionally. When the mixture has achieved the desired sweetness, stop adding the dates and blend until smooth.

Place the blender in the freezer for 40 minutes to 1 hour or in the refrigerator for at least 1 hour or up to overnight, until well chilled. Pour the mixture into an ice cream maker and freeze according to the manufacturer's instructions. Serve immediately or transfer to airtight containers and store in the freezer until ready to serve.

Piña Colada

2¼ pounds organic Sugar Loaf pineapple, cut into 1-inch chunks
1 cup packed organic pitted honey dates (see page 6)
2 cups fresh coconut milk (see page 11)

Run the pineapple through a juicer to make 2 cups of juice.

Combine the pineapple juice and dates in a blender. Blend on high until silky smooth, at least 1 minute. If the mixture seems too thick and is difficult to blend, add a little of the coconut milk and blend until smooth. Add the remaining coconut milk and blend again until smooth.

Place the blender in the freezer for 40 minutes to 1 hour or in the refrigerator for at least 1 hour or up to overnight, until well chilled. Pour the mixture into an ice cream maker and freeze according to the manufacturer's instructions. Serve immediately or transfer to airtight containers and store in the freezer until ready to serve.

Hazelnut Cherry
MAKES ABOUT 1 QUART

2 cups hazelnut milk (page 10)
½ cup packed organic pitted medjool dates (see page 6)
2 cups packed organic pitted Bing, Lambert, or Rainier cherries

Combine the hazelnut milk, dates, and 1 cup of the cherries in a blender. Blend on high until silky smooth, at least 1 minute. Place the blender in the freezer for 40 minutes to 1 hour or in the refrigerator for at least 1 hour or up to overnight, until well chilled.

Chop the remaining 1 cup cherries and place in the freezer to chill.

Pour the hazelnut-cherry mixture into an ice cream maker and freeze according to the manufacturer's instructions. Remove the cover and blade from the ice cream maker and fold in the chopped cherries, distributing evenly. Serve immediately or transfer to airtight containers and store in the freezer until ready to serve.

Banana Almond

MAKES ABOUT 1 QUART

2 cups almond milk (page 10)
2 cups mashed overripe organic bananas

Combine the almond milk and bananas in a blender. Blend on high until silky smooth, at least 1 minute.

Place the blender in the freezer for 40 minutes to 1 hour or in the refrigerator for at least 1 hour or up to overnight, until well chilled. Pour the mixture into an ice cream maker and freeze according to the manufacturer's instructions. Serve immediately or transfer to airtight containers and store in the freezer until ready to serve.

Raw Vanilla

MAKES ABOUT 1 QUART

2 vanilla beans
2½ cups young coconut water (see page 10)
1 cup raw organic cashews or cashew pieces
¾ cup packed organic pitted honey dates (see page 6)

Cut the vanilla beans into small pieces. Grind to a fine powder in a clean coffee grinder.

Combine the ground vanilla, coconut water, and cashews in a blender. Blend on high until silky smooth, at least 1 minute. With the motor running, gradually add the dates and blend until smooth.

Place the blender in the freezer for 40 minutes to 1 hour or in the refrigerator for at least 1 hour or up to overnight, until well chilled. Pour the mixture into an ice cream maker and freeze according to the manufacturer's instructions. Serve immediately or transfer to airtight containers and store in the freezer until ready to serve.

Vanilla Hazelnut

MAKES ABOUT 1 QUART

2 vanilla beans
2½ cups hazelnut milk (page 10)
1½ cups packed organic pitted honey dates (see page 6)

Cut the vanilla beans into small pieces. Grind to a fine powder in a clean coffee grinder.

Combine the ground vanilla, hazelnut milk, and dates in a blender. Blend on high until silky smooth, at least 1 minute.

Place the blender in the freezer for 40 minutes to 1 hour or in the refrigerator for at least 1 hour or up to overnight, until well chilled. Pour the mixture into an ice cream maker and freeze according to the manufacturer's instructions. Serve immediately or transfer to airtight containers and store in the freezer until ready to serve.

Coconut Vanilla

MAKES ABOUT 1 QUART

3 vanilla beans
3 cups fresh coconut milk (see page 11)
1 cup packed organic pitted medjool dates (see page 6)

Cut the vanilla beans into small pieces. Grind to a fine powder in a clean coffee grinder.

Combine the ground vanilla, coconut milk, and dates in a blender. Blend on high until silky smooth, at least 1 minute.

Place the blender in the freezer for 40 minutes to 1 hour or in the refrigerator for at least 1 hour or up to overnight, until well chilled. Pour the mixture into an ice cream maker and freeze according to the manufacturer's instructions. Serve immediately or transfer to airtight containers and store in the freezer until ready to serve.

Almond Date

MAKES ABOUT 1 QUART

3 cups almond milk (page 10)
1 cup packed organic pitted honey dates (see page 6)

Combine the almond milk and dates in a blender. Blend on high until silky smooth, at least 1 minute.

Place the blender in the freezer for 40 minutes to 1 hour or in the refrigerator for at least 1 hour or up to overnight, until well chilled. Pour the mixture into an ice cream maker and freeze according to the manufacturer's instructions. Serve immediately or transfer to airtight containers and store in the freezer until ready to serve.

Raw Carob

2½ cups coconut water (see page 10)
1 cup raw organic cashews or cashew pieces
¾ cup packed organic pitted honey dates (see page 6)
½ cup unsweetened carob powder

Combine the coconut water and cashews in a blender. Blend on high until silky smooth, at least 1 minute. Add the dates and continue blending until smooth. With the motor running, add the carob powder and blend until evenly distributed.

Place the blender in the freezer for 40 minutes to 1 hour or in the refrigerator for at least 1 hour or up to overnight, until well chilled. Pour the mixture into an ice cream maker and freeze according to the manufacturer's instructions. Serve immediately or transfer to airtight containers and store in the freezer until ready to serve.

Coconut Carob

3 cups fresh coconut milk (see page 11)
1 cup packed organic pitted black dates (see page 6)
½ cup unsweetened carob powder

Combine the coconut milk and dates in a blender. Blend on high until silky smooth, at least 1 minute. With the motor running, add the carob powder and blend until evenly distributed.

Place the blender in the freezer for 40 minutes to 1 hour or in the refrigerator for at least 1 hour or up to overnight, until well chilled. Pour the mixture into an ice cream maker and freeze according to the manufacturer's instructions. Serve immediately or transfer to airtight containers and store in the freezer until ready to serve.

Almond Carob Replace the coconut milk with 3 cups almond milk (page 10).

Raw Black Forest

MAKES ABOUT 1 QUART

¾ cup packed organic pitted black dates
¾ cup purified water or coconut water (see page 10)
1¾ pounds organic Bing, Lambert, or Rainier cherries, pitted,
*   plus 1 cup chopped pitted cherries*
1 cup raw organic cashews or cashew pieces
½ cup unsweetened carob powder

Place the dates in a jar and add the purified the water. Refrigerate overnight. Drain, reserving the sweet soaking liquid.

Run the 1¾ pounds cherries through a juicer to make 2 cups of juice.

Combine the cherry juice, cashews, and dates and their soaking liquid in a blender. Blend on high until silky smooth, at least 1 minute. With the motor running, add the carob powder and blend until evenly distributed. Place the blender in the freezer for 40 minutes to 1 hour or in the refrigerator for at least 1 hour or up to overnight, until well chilled.

Place the chopped cherries in the freezer to chill.

Pour the cherry juice mixture into an ice cream maker and freeze according to the manufacturer's instructions. Remove the cover and blade from the ice cream maker and fold in the chopped cherries, distributing evenly. Serve immediately or transfer to airtight containers and store in the freezer until ready to serve.

Pecan Pie

1 vanilla bean
1 cup chopped organic pecans
3 cups pecan milk (page 10)
1 cup packed organic pitted honey dates (see page 6)

Cut the vanilla bean into small pieces. Grind to a fine powder in a clean coffee grinder. Place the chopped pecans in the freezer to chill.

Combine the ground vanilla, pecan milk, and dates in a blender. Blend on high until silky smooth, at least 1 minute.

Place the blender in the freezer for 40 minutes to 1 hour or in the refrigerator for at least 1 hour or up to overnight, until well chilled. Pour the mixture into an ice cream maker and freeze according to the manufacturer's instructions. Remove the cover and blade from the ice cream maker and fold in the chopped pecans, distributing evenly. Serve immediately or transfer to airtight containers and store in the freezer until ready to serve.

Vegg Nog

MAKES ABOUT 1 QUART

1 vanilla bean
3 cups fresh coconut milk (see page 11)
⅔ cup packed organic pitted honey dates (see page 6)
¼ teaspoon ground nutmeg
⅔ cup mashed slightly overripe organic banana

Cut the vanilla bean into small pieces. Grind to a fine powder in a clean coffee grinder.

Combine the ground vanilla, coconut milk, dates, and nutmeg in a blender. Blend on high until silky smooth, at least 1 minute. Add the banana and continue blending until creamy.

Place the blender in the freezer for 40 minutes to 1 hour or in the refrigerator for at least 1 hour or up to overnight, until well chilled. Pour the mixture into an ice cream maker and freeze according to the manufacturer's instructions. Serve immediately or transfer to airtight containers and store in the freezer until ready to serve.

Raw Gingersnap

MAKES ABOUT 1 QUART

3 cups almond milk (page 10)
1 cup packed organic pitted black dates (see page 6)
2 tablespoons fresh organic ginger juice (see page 9)

Combine the almond milk, dates, and ginger juice in a blender. Blend on high until silky smooth, at least 1 minute.

Place the blender in the freezer for 40 minutes to 1 hour or in the refrigerator for at least 1 hour or up to overnight, until well chilled. Pour the mixture into an ice cream maker and freeze according to the manufacturer's instructions. Serve immediately or transfer to airtight containers and store in the freezer until ready to serve.

Chai

2½ cups coconut water (see page 10)
1 cup raw organic cashews or cashew pieces
2 teaspoons minced organic ginger
½ teaspoon ground cardamom
¼ teaspoon ground cloves
¼ teaspoon ground cinnamon
¼ teaspoon ground allspice
¾ cup packed organic pitted honey dates (see page 6)

Combine the coconut water, cashews, ginger, cardamom, cloves, cinnamon, and allspice in a blender. Blend on high until silky smooth, at least 1 minute. Add the dates and continue blending until smooth.

Place the blender in the freezer for 40 minutes to 1 hour or in the refrigerator for at least 1 hour or up to overnight, until well chilled. Pour the mixture into an ice cream maker and freeze according to the manufacturer's instructions. Serve immediately or transfer to airtight containers and store in the freezer until ready to serve.

Raw Jalapeño Heaven

MAKES ABOUT 1 QUART

1 to 3 teaspoons minced organic jalapeño chile
3 cups purified water
1 cup raw organic cashews or cashew pieces
1 cup packed organic pitted medjool dates (see page 6)

Combine the jalapeño, water, and cashews in a blender. Just
1 teaspoon of jalapeño will give the vice cream a slight flavor with a
little kick. Adding a second teaspoon will give you more heat, and
3 teaspoons will deliver quite a punch. Blend on high until silky
smooth, at least 1 minute. Add the dates and continue blending until
smooth.

Place the blender in the freezer for 40 minutes to 1 hour or in the
refrigerator for at least 1 hour or up to overnight, until well chilled.
Pour the mixture into an ice cream maker and freeze according to the
manufacturer's instructions. Serve immediately or transfer to airtight
containers and store in the freezer until ready to serve.

Sauces

Carob Sauce

MAKES ABOUT 2½ CUPS

½ cup organic cashews or cashew pieces
1½ cups coconut water (see page 10), plus more as needed
½ cup packed organic pitted honey dates (see page 6)
¾ cup carob powder

Combine the cashews and coconut water in a blender. Blend on high until silky smooth, at least 1 minute. Add the dates and blend until smooth. (Dates vary in water content, so you may need to add more coconut water to achieve a smooth consistency.) Add the carob powder and blend until evenly distributed. Serve over the vice cream of your choice. (Store refrigerated, in an airtight container, for up to 3 days.)

Coconut Sauce

⅔ cup fresh coconut milk (see page 11)
⅓ cup packed organic pitted honey dates (see page 6)

Combine the coconut milk and dates in a blender. A 1-cup blender jar works best. Blend on high until silky smooth, at least 1 minute. Serve over the vice cream of your choice. (Store refrigerated, in an airtight container, for up to 3 days.)

Strawberry Sauce

MAKES 1 CUP

1½ cups packed hulled organic strawberries
⅓ cup packed organic pitted honey dates (see page 6)

Run the strawberries through a juicer to make ⅔ cup of juice. Alternatively, you can purée the strawberries in a blender.

Combine the strawberry juice and dates in a blender. A 1-cup blender jar works best. Blend on high until silky smooth, at least 1 minute. Serve over the vice cream of your choice. (Store refrigerated, in an airtight container, for up to 3 days.)

Strawberry Sauce Too

MAKES I CUP

½ cup packed hulled organic strawberries
¼ cup packed organic pitted honey dates (see page 6)
¼ cup coconut water (see page 10), plus more as needed

Combine the strawberries, dates, and coconut water in a blender. A 1-cup blender jar works best. Blend on high until silky smooth, at least 1 minute. (Dates vary in water content, so you may need to add more coconut water to achieve a smooth consistency.) Serve over the vice cream of your choice. (Store refrigerated, in an airtight container, for up to 3 days.)

Raspberry Sauce

MAKES 1 CUP

¼ cup packed organic raspberries
¼ cup packed organic pitted honey dates (see page 6)
½ cup coconut water (see page 10) or purified water, plus more
   as needed

Combine the raspberries, dates, and coconut water in a blender.
A 1-cup blender jar works best. Blend on high until silky smooth,
at least 1 minute. (Dates vary in water content, so you may need to
add more coconut water to achieve a smooth consistency.) Serve over
the vice cream of your choice. (Store refrigerated, in an airtight container, for up to 3 days.)

Blueberry Sauce

MAKES 1 CUP

1½ cups organic blueberries
⅓ cup packed organic pitted honey dates (see page 6)

Run the blueberries through a juicer to make ⅔ cup of juice. Alternatively, you can blend the blueberries without juicing.

Combine the blueberry juice and dates in a blender. A 1-cup blender jar works best. Blend on high until silky smooth, at least 1 minute. Serve over the vice cream of your choice. (Store refrigerated, in an airtight container, for up to 3 days.)

Mango Sauce

MAKES 1 CUP

1½ cups sliced peeled organic mango
⅓ cup packed organic pitted honey dates (see page 6)

Run the mango through a juicer to make ⅔ cup of juice. Alternatively, you can blend the mango without juicing.

Combine the mango juice and dates in a blender. A 1-cup blender jar works best. Blend on high until silky smooth, at least 1 minute. Serve over the vice cream of your choice. (Store refrigerated, in an airtight container, for up to 3 days.)

ABOUT THE AUTHOR

Jeff Rogers grew up in Stowe, Vermont, where he became interested in food and tourism. After working at a popular restaurant, he moved to

New Hampshire to study hotel and restaurant management at college. While pursuing a career in hotels, he honed his skills in the kitchen by experimenting and creating recipes of his own.

Adapting his diet to improve his health, he eventually became a vegan, eschewing all animal products. But he still craved the premium dairy ice creams he once ate, and so used his kitchen gifts to experiment with creating a rich, gourmet vegan ice cream: vice cream. As he became interested in the raw food movement, he also began to make vice creams with all raw ingredients.

Soon after beginning his vice cream venture, Jeff began sharing his desserts with friends. A physician friend noted that in a world where people are trying to eat low-fat foods and fewer sweets, it was naughty of Jeff to create these decadent desserts, vegan or not. Thus, he was dubbed the Naughty Vegan and has used the nickname ever since.

You can learn more about Jeff and his vice cream by visiting his website, www.TheNaughtyVegan.com. He is also a co-founder of SoyStache.com, a nonprofit project that promotes awareness of the many benefits of a plant-based diet. He currently lives in Seattle, Washington.

INDEX